How to Conduct Market Research Effectively

A Guide to Efficient Market Research for Competitiveness and Business Growth

G. Dellis

Copyright © 2024

How to Conduct Market Research Effectively

1. Introduction

Introduction to Market Research: How to Do It Effectively

1. What is Market Research?

Market research is a systematic process aimed at collecting, analyzing, and interpreting information related to a market, product, or service. This process is crucial for understanding the needs, preferences, and behaviors of consumers, as well as identifying market trends, evaluating competition, and developing effective marketing strategies.

2. Importance of Market Research

2.1 Risk Reduction

Market research helps companies make informed decisions, reducing the risk of launching products or services that might not succeed. Knowing the market and target audience allows for tailoring the offering to the specific needs of consumers.

2.2 Understanding Consumers

Through research, it is possible to gain a deep understanding of consumers' preferences, behaviors, and motivations. This enables the creation of more targeted and effective marketing strategies.

2.3 Identifying Opportunities

Market research can reveal new business opportunities, such as untapped market niches or potential areas of growth. This allows companies to innovate and remain competitive.

2.4 Evaluating Competition

Analyzing the competition is essential to understand how one's products or services are positioned relative to competitors. This helps identify strengths and weaknesses and develop strategies to differentiate.

3. Types of Market Research

3.1 Primary Research

Primary research involves collecting original data directly from the market through methods such as surveys, interviews, focus groups, and observations. This type of research is specific and can be tailored to the particular needs of the company.

3.1.1 Surveys

Surveys are one of the most common tools for collecting primary data. They can be conducted online, by phone, or in person, and allow for gathering quantitative and qualitative information on a wide range of topics.

3.1.2 Interviews

Interviews provide more detailed and in-depth information compared to surveys. They can be conducted individually or in groups and can be structured, semi-structured, or unstructured.

3.1.3 Focus Groups

Focus groups consist of guided discussions with a small group of people from the target audience. This method allows for deep exploration of opinions and perceptions.

3.1.4 Observations

Direct observation of consumer behavior in real or simulated contexts provides valuable data on how they interact with products and services.

3.2 Secondary Research

Secondary research uses existing data collected from other sources such as industry reports, academic studies, government statistics, and newspaper articles. This type of research is less expensive and quicker than primary research but may not be as specific.

3.2.1 Public Sources

Public sources, such as government statistics

and reports from international agencies, provide reliable and accessible data.

3.2.2 Commercial Sources

Commercial sources include market research reports published by specialized companies. These reports offer detailed analyses but can be costly.

3.2.3 Internal Sources

Internal company data, such as historical sales records, customer reports, and feedback, are valuable resources for market research.

4. Steps in Market Research

4.1 Defining Objectives

Before starting the research, it is essential to establish specific objectives that you want to achieve. These objectives will guide the entire research process.

4.2 Research Design

The design phase involves choosing the most appropriate methods and tools for data collection. It is important to decide whether to conduct primary, secondary research, or a combination of both.

4.3 Data Collection

This phase involves the actual collection of information through the chosen methods. The quality of the collected data is crucial for the accuracy and reliability of the conclusions.

4.4 Data Analysis

Collected data must be analyzed to identify trends, patterns, and relevant information. The analysis can be quantitative, qualitative, or a combination of both.

4.5 Interpretation and Reporting

The results of the analysis must be interpreted and presented clearly and understandably. It is important to highlight the practical implications of the findings and provide data-based recommendations.

4.6 Implementing Findings

The information obtained from the research must be used to make strategic and operational decisions. This may include product adjustments, modifying marketing strategies, or identifying new market opportunities.

5. Research Methodologies

5.1 Quantitative Methods

Quantitative methods are based on numerical and statistical data. They are useful for obtaining general and measurable information about the market and consumers. Examples include surveys and sales data analysis.

5.2 Qualitative Methods

Qualitative methods focus on descriptive and

in-depth data. They provide a more detailed understanding of consumer motivations and perceptions. Examples include in-depth interviews and focus groups.

6. Technological Tools for Market Research

6.1 Online Survey Software

Platforms such as SurveyMonkey, Google Forms, and Qualtrics allow for creating and distributing online surveys, collecting data efficiently, and automatically analyzing it.

6.2 Social Media Analysis

Tools such as Hootsuite, Sprout Social, and Brandwatch help monitor and analyze social media conversations, providing valuable insights into consumer opinions and market trends.

6.3 Big Data Analysis

Big data analysis uses advanced algorithms to analyze large amounts of data from various sources, such as online transactions and sensor data, to identify patterns and trends.

7. Challenges in Market Research

7.1 Data Bias

Bias can affect research results, compromising the accuracy of conclusions. It is important to design the research to minimize bias and use representative samples.

7.2 Changes in Consumer Behavior

Consumer behaviors can change rapidly, making data obsolete. It is crucial to conduct regular research to keep information up-to-date.

7.3 Privacy and Ethics

The collection and use of consumer data must comply with privacy regulations and ethical guidelines. It is important to obtain informed consent and protect sensitive data.

Market research is an essential tool for companies that want to understand their market and consumers, identify growth opportunities, and develop effective marketing strategies. A well-planned and rigorously conducted research process provides valuable data that can guide informed business decisions and reduce the risks associated with launching new products or services.

Investing in market research not only helps meet consumer needs but also contributes to building a sustainable competitive advantage, allowing companies to quickly adapt to market changes and maintain a leadership position in their sector.

2. Defining Research Objectives

Defining research objectives is a crucial preliminary phase in the market research process. Establishing clear and well-defined objectives helps guide the entire research project, ensuring resources are used effectively and that the results obtained are relevant and useful for the company. This document will explore in detail the importance of research objectives, how to define them effectively, and the different types of objectives that can be pursued in market research.

2. The Importance of Defining Research Objectives

2.1 Guiding the Research Project

Research objectives provide a clear direction for the entire research project. By defining what you want to discover or understand, you can outline the most appropriate methodologies, choose the right tools, and set the subsequent phases of the project coherently.

2.2 Optimizing Resources

Establishing specific objectives helps use resources more efficiently. Without clear objectives, there's a risk of collecting unnecessary or irrelevant data, wasting time and money. Well-defined objectives allow focusing research efforts on the most important and relevant areas.

2.3 Evaluating Results

With well-defined objectives, it is easier to evaluate the success of the research. Objectives serve as evaluation criteria to determine if the results obtained answer the research questions and meet the company's needs.

2.4 Clear Communication

Research objectives facilitate communication among various stakeholders involved in the project. Managers, researchers, and other interested parties can have a shared understanding of the research purposes, reducing the risk of misunderstandings and ensuring effective collaboration.

3. The Process of Defining Research Objectives

3.1 Context Analysis

Before defining objectives, it is essential to understand the context in which the company operates. This includes analyzing the market, competitors, industry trends, and consumer needs. A solid understanding of the context helps identify critical areas that need further investigation.

3.2 Identifying Informational Needs

The informational needs of the company must be clearly identified. This involves understanding what information is necessary for making strategic decisions, what problems need to be solved, and what opportunities need to be explored.

3.3 Formulating Objectives

Research objectives should be formulated to be specific, measurable, achievable, relevant, and time-bound (SMART). A good research objective should answer the following questions:

- **Specific**: What exactly do we want to discover?

- **Measurable**: How will we measure success?

- **Achievable**: Is it realistic to achieve this objective with the resources available?

- **Relevant**: Is the objective pertinent to business decisions?

- **Time-bound**: What is the deadline for achieving the objective?

3.4 Prioritizing Objectives

Not all objectives have the same importance. It is necessary to prioritize objectives based on their strategic relevance and potential impact on business outcomes. This helps focus on the most critical aspects of the research.

4. Types of Research Objectives

4.1 Exploratory Objectives

Exploratory objectives are used when there is limited knowledge of the research problem, and a preliminary understanding is desired. These objectives are often formulated to identify new market opportunities, explore emerging consumer behaviors, or understand the dynamics of a little-known market.

Examples:

- Explore consumer motivations for purchasing eco-friendly products.

- Identify emerging trends in the wearable technology market.

4.2 Descriptive Objectives

Descriptive objectives aim to provide a detailed description of a phenomenon or market situation. These objectives are often used to quantify market sizes, consumer demographic profiles, or customer satisfaction levels.

Examples:

- Describe the demographic profile of consumers for a new food product.

- Quantify customer satisfaction levels regarding a technical support service.

4.3 Causal Objectives

Causal objectives seek to establish cause-and-effect relationships between variables. These objectives are useful for testing specific hypotheses and understanding how certain changes or interventions can influence consumer behaviors or market performance.

Examples:

- Determine the effect of an advertising campaign on product sales.

- Analyze the impact of price on the perception of service quality.

5. Practical Examples of Defining Objectives

5.1 Launching a New Product

Context: A cosmetics company is about to launch a new line of organic products.

Informational Needs:

- Understand consumer preferences for organic products.

- Identify the acceptable price for the target market.

- Evaluate the competition in the organic cosmetics segment.

Research Objectives:

- Explore consumer motivations for purchasing organic cosmetics (Exploratory).

- Describe the demographic and psychographic profile of the target market for organic cosmetics (Descriptive).

- Determine the effect of price on the perception of quality of organic cosmetics (Causal).

5.2 Improving Customer Service

Context: A telecommunications service company wants to improve its customer service.

Informational Needs:

- Measure the current level of customer satisfaction.

- Identify critical points in customer service that need improvement.

- Evaluate the impact of improvement initiatives on customer satisfaction levels.

Research Objectives:

- Quantify the current level of customer satisfaction (Descriptive).

- Explore the main causes of customer dissatisfaction (Exploratory).

- Analyze the effect of new improvement initiatives on customer satisfaction (Causal).

6. Tools for Defining Objectives

6.1 Brainstorming

Brainstorming is an effective method for generating ideas and identifying research objectives. Involving various team members can provide diverse perspectives and identify key areas of interest.

6.2 SWOT Analysis

SWOT analysis (Strengths, Weaknesses, Opportunities, Threats) helps understand the internal and external context of the company, identifying key areas to focus on. This analysis can guide the definition of relevant research objectives.

6.3 SMART Model

Using the SMART model (Specific, Measurable, Achievable, Relevant, Time-bound) ensures that research objectives are clear and achievable. This model is particularly useful for avoiding vague or unrealistic objectives.

6.4 Prioritization Matrix

The prioritization matrix helps rank objectives based on their importance and potential impact. This tool allows focusing on the most critical and relevant objectives for the company.

7. Challenges in Defining Research Objectives

7.1 Too Broad or Generic Objectives

Objectives that are too broad or generic can make the research dispersed and unfocused. It is important to define specific and circumscribed objectives to obtain useful and concrete results.

7.2 Lack of Consensus Among Stakeholders

Lack of consensus among various stakeholders can lead to conflicting or unclear objectives. Involving all interested parties in the objective-setting phase is crucial to ensure shared adherence.

7.3 Changes in Market Context

The market context can change rapidly, rendering some research objectives obsolete. It is important to remain flexible and ready to adapt objectives in response to market changes.

7.4 Limited Resources

Limited resources in terms of time, budget, and personnel can make it difficult to achieve all desired objectives. Prioritizing objectives and strategically allocating resources is crucial to overcoming this challenge.

8. Conclusion

Defining research objectives is a fundamental phase in the market research process. Clear, specific, and well-formulated objectives guide the entire research project, ensuring resources are used effectively and the results obtained are relevant and useful for the company. Using tools such as the SMART model, brainstorming, and SWOT analysis can facilitate the definition of relevant and achievable objectives.

A well-structured objective-setting process not only contributes to the success of the research project but also provides a solid foundation for making informed strategic decisions, reducing risk, and increasing the chances of market success. Investing time and energy in the objective-setting phase is therefore an indispensable step for any company that wishes to better understand its market and fully exploit the opportunities it offers.

3. Identification of the Target Audience in Market Research

1. Introduction

Identifying the target audience is a crucial phase in market research and the formulation of marketing strategies. Knowing your target audience allows companies to develop products, services, and communication campaigns that effectively meet the needs, preferences, and behaviors of consumers. This document will explore in detail the importance of identifying the target audience, the methods for doing so, and how to use the information obtained to improve business strategies.

2. Importance of Identifying the Target Audience

2.1 Improvement of Marketing Strategies

Identifying the target audience enables the development of more targeted and personalized marketing strategies. Knowing your audience allows you to create messages that resonate with their needs and desires, increasing the effectiveness of promotional campaigns.

2.2 Optimization of Resources

Focusing marketing efforts on a specific target helps optimize company resources. Instead of wasting time and money on a broad and generic audience, companies can concentrate their resources on more profitable market segments with higher conversion probabilities.

2.3 Development of Suitable Products and Services

Knowing the target audience allows companies to develop products and services that precisely meet consumer needs. This not only increases customer satisfaction but also the likelihood of the product or service's success in the market.

2.4 Improvement of Customer Relationships

Understanding who your customers are enables the establishment of stronger and more lasting relationships with them. Companies can offer more personalized service, anticipating customer needs and responding promptly to their requests.

3. Stages of Identifying the Target Audience

3.1 Information Gathering

The first phase involves gathering information about potential consumers. This can be done through primary and secondary research methods such as surveys, interviews, focus groups, demographic data analysis, and existing market research.

3.1.1 Primary Research

Primary research involves collecting data directly from consumers through various tools:

- **Surveys**: Useful for collecting quantitative data from a large sample of consumers.

- **Interviews**: Allow for detailed and qualitative information on consumer behaviors and preferences.

- **Focus Groups**: Provide in-depth analysis of consumer opinions and perceptions on specific products or services.

- **Observations**: Direct observation of consumer behavior in real contexts offers valuable insights.

3.1.2 Secondary Research

Secondary research uses existing data collected from other sources:

- **Industry Reports**: Provide an overview of market trends and competitive dynamics.

- **Government Statistics**: Offer relevant demographic and socioeconomic data.

- **Academic Studies**: Contribute theoretical and empirical analyses of consumer behavior.

- **Competitor Analysis**: Provide information on market segments served by competitors and their strategies.

3.2 Market Segmentation

Once the information is gathered, the next step is to segment the market. Segmentation involves dividing the overall market into distinct groups of consumers with similar characteristics and behaviors.

3.2.1 Segmentation Criteria

The main segmentation criteria include:

- **Demographic**: Age, gender, income, education level, marital status, family size.

- **Geographic**: Region, city, climate, population density.

- **Psychographic**: Lifestyle, personality, values, interests.

- **Behavioral**: Buying habits, brand loyalty, usage frequency, usage occasions.

3.3 Segment Analysis

After segmenting the market, each segment needs to be analyzed to assess its potential.

This analysis includes:

- **Segment Size and Growth**: Assessing how many consumers belong to the segment and its growth rate.

- **Segment Attractiveness**: Analyzing potential profitability, competition, and entry barriers.

- **Compatibility with the Company**: Evaluating if the segment aligns with the company's mission, resources, and capabilities.

3.4 Target Selection

Once the segments are analyzed, the company must choose the target audience. There are several targeting strategies:

- **Undifferentiated Targeting**: The company decides not to segment the market and offers the same product to all consumers.

- **Differentiated Targeting**: The company chooses to serve different market segments with specific offers for each segment.

- **Concentrated Targeting**: The company focuses on a single market segment, dedicating all resources to meeting the needs of that segment.

- **Micromarketing**: The company customizes its offer for very small or individual segments.

3.5 Target Profiling

The final phase involves creating a detailed profile of the target audience. This profile includes demographic, psychographic, behavioral, and geographic information, as well as insights into consumer needs, motivations, and expectations.

4. Methods for Identifying the Target Audience

4.1 Demographic Data Analysis

Demographic data analysis is one of the first steps in identifying the target audience. This analysis includes examining variables such as age, gender, income, education level, occupation, and family structure.

Usage Examples:

- A toy company might focus on families with young children.

- A luxury goods manufacturer might target consumers with high incomes.

4.2 Psychographic Analysis

Psychographic analysis goes beyond demographic data to examine consumers' psychological traits, such as values, attitudes, interests, and lifestyles.

Usage Examples:

- A sportswear company might segment the market based on active lifestyles and a passion for sports.

- An organic food producer might target consumers with strong ecological values and health consciousness.

4.3 Behavioral Analysis

Behavioral analysis focuses on consumer buying and product usage habits. It includes analyzing purchase frequency, brand loyalty, and usage occasions.

Usage Examples:

- A coffee company might identify consumers who drink coffee daily versus those who consume it occasionally.

- An online retailer might segment customers based on their purchase frequency and average order value.

4.4 Geographic Analysis

Geographic analysis divides the market based on the consumers' geographic location. It includes variables such as region, city, climate, and population density.

Usage Examples:

- A clothing company might develop product lines specific to hot or cold climates.

- A food delivery service might focus on urban areas with high population density.

4.5 Big Data Analysis

Big data analysis uses advanced technologies to collect and analyze large amounts of data from various sources, such as social media, online transactions, and IoT sensors. This analysis provides detailed insights into consumer behaviors and preferences.

Usage Examples:

- An online retailer could use browsing and purchase data to personalize offers to customers.

- An auto manufacturer could analyze vehicle sensor data to understand driving habits and improve products.

5. Tools and Technologies for Identifying the Target Audience

5.1 CRM Software

Customer Relationship Management (CRM) software helps companies collect and analyze customer data, manage interactions with them, and improve retention.

Advantages:

- Centralization of customer data.

- Personalization of communications and offers.

- Analysis of customer trends and behaviors.

5.2 Social Media Analysis Platforms

Social media analysis platforms allow for monitoring and analyzing conversations and interactions on social networks, providing valuable insights into consumer preferences and behaviors.

Advantages:

- Real-time monitoring of trends and opinions.

- Identification of influencers and brand ambassadors.

- Analysis of sentiment and brand perceptions.

5.3 Web Analytics Tools

Web analytics tools, such as Google Analytics, allow for analyzing website traffic and online user behavior, providing detailed information on their navigation paths and preferences.

Advantages:

- Monitoring key website metrics (e.g., traffic, conversion rate).

- Analysis of user behavior (e.g., pages visited, time spent).

- Segmentation of users based on demographic and behavioral variables.

5.4 Business Intelligence Software

Business Intelligence (BI) software aggregates and analyzes data from various business sources, providing detailed dashboards and reports to support strategic decisions.

Advantages:

- Real-time data visualization and analysis.

- Identification of trends and behavior patterns.

- Data-driven decision support.

5.5 Big Data Analysis Tools

Big data analysis tools, such as Hadoop and Spark, allow for managing and analyzing large volumes of heterogeneous data, providing in-depth insights into consumers.

Advantages:

- Analysis of structured and unstructured data.

- Scalability and real-time processing capabilities.

- Identification of complex patterns and hidden relationships.

6. Practical Examples of Identifying the Target Audience

6.1 Case Study: Sportswear Company

Context: A sportswear company wants to launch a new fitness clothing line.

Methodology:

- **Primary Research**: Surveys and interviews with fitness enthusiasts.

- **Market Segmentation**: Psychographic segmentation based on active lifestyle and sports interests.

- **Segment Analysis**: Evaluation of the size and growth of the active fitness consumer segment.

- **Target Selection**: Focus on consumers aged 18-35 with an active lifestyle and interest in fitness.

- **Target Profiling**: Creation of detailed profiles including demographic, psychographic, and behavioral data.

Results:

- **Product Development**: Creation of functional and stylish fitness clothing.

- **Marketing Strategies**: Social media advertising and sponsorship of sports events to reach the target.

- **Personalized Offers**: Special promotions and discounts for gym and sports club members.

6.2 Case Study: Food Delivery Service

Context: A food delivery service wants to expand into new urban areas.

Methodology:

- **Secondary Research**: Analysis of

industry reports and demographic statistics of new urban areas.

- **Market Segmentation**: Geographic and behavioral segmentation based on population density and food delivery consumption habits.

- **Segment Analysis**: Evaluation of the attractiveness of urban areas in terms of potential demand and competition.

- **Target Selection**: Identification of urban areas with high population density and a tendency to use food delivery services.

- **Target Profiling**: Creation of detailed profiles including geographic and behavioral data.

Results:

- **Service Expansion**: Launch of the service in new urban areas with high demand.

- **Marketing Strategies**: Local digital marketing campaigns and partnerships with popular restaurants in the new areas.

- **Personalized Offers**: Special offers for new customers and loyalty programs for repeat customers.

7. Conclusion

Identifying the target audience is an essential process in market research and business strategy development. Through a structured approach that includes information gathering, market segmentation, segment analysis, target selection, and target profiling, companies can better understand their consumers and meet their needs effectively. Utilizing modern tools and technologies can further enhance this process, providing detailed and actionable insights into consumer behavior. In the end, a precise understanding of the target audience allows companies to develop more effective marketing strategies, optimize resources, create suitable products and services, and establish strong and lasting relationships with their customers.

4. Choosing Research Methodology and Data Collection and Analysis

Choosing the research methodology and subsequently collecting and analyzing data are fundamental steps in market research. These steps determine the quality and reliability of the gathered information, which in turn influence the company's strategic decisions. This document will explore in detail the various available methodological approaches, data collection processes, and analysis techniques to ensure accurate and useful results.

2. Choosing the Research Methodology

2.1 Types of Research

There are two main categories of market research: primary research and secondary research.

2.1.1 Primary Research

Primary research involves collecting original data directly from the source. This type of research is particularly useful when the required information is not available through existing sources.

Examples of Primary Research Methodologies:

- **Surveys**: Questionnaires administered to a representative sample of the target audience.

- **Interviews**: In-depth conversations with selected individuals to obtain qualitative insights.

- **Focus Groups**: Guided discussions with small groups of people to explore opinions and perceptions.

- **Observation**: Monitoring consumer behavior in real-life situations.

2.1.2 Secondary Research

Secondary research utilizes data already collected from other sources. This approach is less expensive and time-consuming than primary research.

Examples of Secondary Research Sources:

- **Industry Reports**: Publications analyzing market trends and competitive dynamics.

- **Government Data**: Official statistics on demographics, economy, and trade.

- **Academic Research**: Studies conducted by research institutions and universities.

- **Internal Data**: Information collected by the company itself, such as sales and customer data.

2.2 Research Methodologies

Depending on the research objectives and the type of data needed, different research methodologies can be adopted.

2.2.1 Quantitative Research

Quantitative research focuses on the collection and analysis of numerical data. It is useful for measuring phenomena and analyzing relationships between variables.

Quantitative Research Methods:

- **Structured Surveys**: Questionnaires with closed-ended questions that allow for the collection of numerical data.

- **Experiments**: Controlled studies that manipulate one or more independent variables to observe the effects on dependent variables.

- **Statistical Analysis**: Use of statistical techniques to analyze collected data and draw conclusions.

2.2.2 Qualitative Research

Qualitative research focuses on understanding consumer behaviors, motivations, and perceptions. It provides richer and more detailed data than quantitative research.

Qualitative Research Methods:

- **In-depth Interviews**: Individual conversations to deeply explore participants' opinions and experiences.

- **Focus Groups**: Group discussions to gather a wide range of opinions on a particular topic.

- **Participant Observation**: The observer immerses themselves in the participants' environment to better understand their behavior.

2.3 Factors to Consider When Choosing a Methodology

2.3.1 Research Objectives

The specific objectives of the research influence the choice of methodology. For instance, if the objective is to measure the extent of a phenomenon, quantitative research is more appropriate. If the goal is to understand the reasons behind certain behaviors, qualitative research is more suitable.

2.3.2 Available Resources

Resources in terms of time, budget, and personnel affect the choice of methodology. Primary research can require significant resources, while secondary research is generally less costly and quicker.

2.3.3 Type of Data Needed

The type of data needed (numerical vs. qualitative) and the depth of information required determine the research methodology. Often, a combination of quantitative and qualitative methods provides a comprehensive view of the research problem.

2.3.4 Accessibility to Participants

The availability and accessibility of participants can limit the choice of methodology. For example, obtaining participants for in-depth interviews can be more challenging than administering online surveys.

3. Data Collection

3.1 Data Collection Methods

3.1.1 Surveys

Surveys are one of the most common tools for collecting quantitative data. They can be administered in various ways, including online, by phone, by mail, or in person.

Advantages:

- Reach a large number of people.

- Can be standardized to ensure consistency.

- Allow for statistical analysis of the collected data.

Disadvantages:

- Potentially inaccurate responses if participants are not truthful.

- Variable response rate.

3.1.2 Interviews

Interviews can be structured, semi-structured,

or unstructured, depending on the desired level of flexibility.

Advantages:

- Provide detailed and in-depth data.
- Allow for immediate clarification.

Disadvantages:

- Require time and resources.
- Can be influenced by interviewer bias.

3.1.3 Focus Groups

Focus groups are guided discussions with a small group of people, generally 6-12 participants, moderated by a facilitator.

Advantages:

- Generate a range of opinions and ideas.

- Allow observation of group dynamics.

Disadvantages:

- Risk of dominance by some participants.
- Difficulty managing the group.

3.1.4 Observation

Observation involves directly monitoring consumer behavior in natural or controlled environments.

Advantages:

- Provides accurate behavioral data.
- Does not require active participation from subjects.

Disadvantages:

- Can be intrusive.

- Difficult to collect detailed data on motivations.

3.2 Data Collection Tools

3.2.1 Questionnaires

Questionnaires are a versatile tool for collecting structured data. They can include closed-ended and open-ended questions and are often used in surveys.

Advantages:

- Easy to distribute and analyze.

- Allow for the collection of standardized data.

Disadvantages:

- Risk of superficial responses.

- Limited capacity for in-depth exploration.

3.2.2 Interview Guides

Interview guides are used to structure semi-structured and unstructured interviews. They include open-ended questions and discussion points to explore topics in depth.

Advantages:

- Flexibility to explore emerging themes.

- Allow for adapting questions based on participant responses.

Disadvantages:

- Require interviewer skills.

- Difficulty in analyzing unstructured responses.

3.2.3 Observation Sheets

Observation sheets are used to systematically record observed behaviors. They can include checklists and rating scales.

Advantages:

- Structure observation to ensure consistency.

- Facilitate the analysis of behavioral data.

Disadvantages:

- Limit flexibility of observation.

- May overlook unanticipated details.

3.3 Ethical Considerations in Data Collection

3.3.1 Informed Consent

Participants must be informed about the research purposes, data collection methods, and their rights. They must provide voluntary consent before participating.

3.3.2 Confidentiality and Anonymity

Collected data must be treated confidentially and anonymized where possible to protect participants' privacy.

3.3.3 Use of Data

Collected data must be used exclusively for the declared research purposes and should not be shared with third parties without participants' consent.

4. Data Analysis

4.1 Data Preparation

4.1.1 Data Cleaning

Before analyzing data, it must be cleaned to remove errors, inconsistencies, and missing values. This process includes verifying data quality and correcting or removing erroneous or incomplete data.

Steps in Data Cleaning:

- **Data Verification**: Check data for entry errors, duplicates, and outliers.

- **Handling Missing Values**: Decide how to treat missing data, e.g., through imputation or deletion.

- **Normalization**: Standardize data to ensure consistency.

4.1.2 Data Coding

Coding is the process of transforming qualitative data into numerical formats to facilitate analysis. This is particularly important for open-ended responses in surveys and interviews.

Examples of Data Coding:

- **Open-ended Responses**: Assign numerical categories to open-ended responses based on recurring themes.

- **Rating Scales**: Transform responses on rating scales into numbers (e.g., from "very dissatisfied" to "very satisfied").

4.2 Quantitative Data Analysis Techniques

4.2.1 Descriptive Analysis

Descriptive analysis provides a summary of the collected data using statistical measures such as means, medians, variances, and percentages.

Examples of Descriptive Analysis:

- **Measures of Central Tendency**: Mean, median, and mode to summarize data.

- **Measures of Dispersion**: Variance, standard deviation, and range to assess data variability.

- **Frequency Distributions**: Tables and charts to represent the distribution of responses.

4.2.2 Inferential Analysis

Inferential analysis allows drawing conclusions about the population based on a sample. It uses statistical tests to verify hypotheses and determine the significance of results.

Examples of Inferential Analysis Techniques:

- **Student's t-test**: Comparing means of two groups.

- **ANOVA**: Analyzing variance to

compare multiple groups.

- **Linear Regression**: Analyzing relationships between independent and dependent variables.

- **Chi-square**: Testing independence between categorical variables.

4.3 Qualitative Data Analysis Techniques

4.3.1 Thematic Analysis

Thematic analysis is a technique used to identify, analyze, and report themes within qualitative data. It involves coding the data and grouping them into recurring themes.

Steps in Thematic Analysis:

- **Initial Coding**: Reading data and assigning initial codes based on emerging concepts.

- **Identifying Themes**: Grouping codes

into broader themes.

- **Reviewing Themes**: Refining identified themes.

- **Defining and Naming Themes**: Clearly defining themes and assigning descriptive names.

4.3.2 Content Analysis

Content analysis is a systematic technique for analyzing textual data. It focuses on quantifying and analyzing keywords, phrases, and ideas within qualitative data.

Steps in Content Analysis:

- **Data Preparation**: Transcribing and organizing data.
- **Coding

**: Identifying and coding relevant content.

- **Quantifying**: Counting occurrences of coded elements.

- **Interpreting Results**: Drawing conclusions based on frequency and context of occurrences.

4.4 Ethical Considerations in Data Analysis

4.4.1 Data Integrity

Researchers must ensure the accuracy and integrity of the data analysis process. Manipulating or misrepresenting data to achieve desired outcomes is unethical.

4.4.2 Transparency

The analysis process should be transparent, and researchers must be open about the methods and procedures used. This includes detailing any limitations or biases that may affect the results.

4.4.3 Confidentiality

The confidentiality of participants must be maintained throughout the analysis process. Data should be anonymized, and access should be restricted to authorized personnel.

4.5 Presenting and Reporting Results

4.5.1 Visual Representation

Visual representation of data, such as charts, graphs, and tables, helps in effectively communicating the results.

Examples of Visual Tools:

- **Bar Charts**: Comparing different

categories.

- **Pie Charts**: Showing proportions within a whole.

- **Line Graphs**: Displaying trends over time.

- **Scatter Plots**: Analyzing relationships between variables.

4.5.2 Written Reports

A comprehensive written report provides a detailed account of the research process, data analysis, and findings. It should include an introduction, methodology, results, discussion, and conclusion sections.

Structure of a Written Report:

- **Introduction**: Background, objectives, and scope of the research.

- **Methodology**: Detailed description of research design and methods used.

- **Results**: Presentation and interpretation of findings.

- **Discussion**: Implications of the results and potential limitations.

- **Conclusion**: Summary of findings and recommendations for future research or actions.

By systematically choosing appropriate methodologies and rigorously collecting and analyzing data, businesses can gain valuable insights into their market and make informed decisions. Ethical considerations must be at the forefront to ensure the integrity and credibility of the research process.

5. Interpretation of Results and Creation of an Effective Service

The interpretation of results and the creation of an effective service represent the final, but crucial, stages in market research. These steps determine how the collected and analyzed data are translated into concrete actions and business strategies. Accurate data interpretation can provide valuable insights, while creating an effective service ensures that customer needs are optimally met. This document will explore in detail how to interpret market research results and how to use these insights to develop a service that meets market needs.

2. Interpretation of Results

2.1 Contextualization of Data

2.1.1 Understanding the Context

Interpreting results must start with understanding the context in which the data were collected. This includes the collection conditions, participant characteristics, and methodological limitations. For example, if a survey was conducted online, it is important to consider that participants might be younger and more technologically savvy than the general population.

2.1.2 Analysis of Contextual Variables

Examining contextual variables that might influence the results is fundamental. These variables include demographic, socioeconomic, cultural, and temporal factors. For instance, an increase in sales during a particular season might be due to seasonal factors rather than changes in consumer behavior.

2.2 Data Triangulation

2.2.1 Combining Methods

Data triangulation involves using multiple data collection and analysis methods to verify the consistency and validity of results. Combining quantitative and qualitative methods can provide a more comprehensive and detailed view of the phenomenon being studied.

2.2.2 Verifying Consistency

Comparing results obtained from different sources and methods can help identify consistent patterns and validate conclusions. For example, if both survey data and qualitative interviews indicate a strong preference for a new product, the validity of the results is strengthened.

2.3 Comparative Analysis

2.3.1 Comparison with Benchmarks

Comparing research results with industry benchmarks or previous studies can help contextualize data and identify significant trends. This comparison can reveal whether a company is performing above or below industry averages.

2.3.2 Trend Analysis

Identifying and analyzing trends over time can provide valuable insights into changes in consumer behavior and market dynamics. For example, a gradual increase in sales of eco-friendly products might indicate a shift in consumer preferences towards more environmentally friendly products.

2.4 Identifying Opportunities

2.4.1 Market Segmentation

Segmenting the market into homogeneous groups of consumers can help identify specific opportunities and tailor marketing strategies. For example, demographic analysis might reveal that young adults are more inclined to purchase advanced technological products.

2.4.2 SWOT Analysis

SWOT analysis (Strengths, Weaknesses, Opportunities, Threats) is a useful tool for assessing market opportunities and threats, as well as the company's strengths and weaknesses. This approach can help identify areas for improvement and develop strategies to leverage emerging opportunities.

2.5 Communication of Results

2.5.1 Reports and Presentations

Research results must be communicated clearly and accessibly. This includes the use of detailed reports and visual presentations that summarize key insights and recommendations. The use of charts, tables, and infographics can facilitate data understanding.

2.5.2 Data Visualization

Data visualization is an effective technique for graphically representing information, making it easier to identify patterns and trends. Tools like interactive dashboards and heat maps can provide an immediate and intuitive view of the results.

2.6 Interpretation and Decision Making

2.6.1 Translating Data into Actions

Interpreting market research results must

culminate in practical and actionable recommendations. This includes identifying specific strategies to improve products, services, and marketing activities.

2.6.2 Validating Decisions

Before implementing decisions based on research results, it is important to validate them through further analysis or pilot tests. This can help ensure that the actions taken are effective and aligned with business objectives.

3. Creation of an Effective Service

3.1 Identifying Customer Needs

3.1.1 Analysis of Customer Feedback

Collecting and analyzing customer feedback is essential for understanding their needs and expectations. This can include analyzing online reviews, social media comments, and customer satisfaction survey results.

3.1.2 Customer Journey Mapping

Customer journey mapping is a technique that allows visualization and analysis of the various stages of the customer journey, from awareness to purchase and beyond. This tool can help identify friction points and opportunities to improve the customer experience.

3.2 Service Development

3.2.1 Service Design

Service design must be based on customer needs and preferences identified through market research. This includes defining service features, pricing structure, distribution channels, and support modalities.

Stages of Service Design:

- **Research and Analysis**: Gather information on customer needs and expectations.

- **Ideation**: Generate ideas for new services or improvements to existing services.

- **Prototyping**: Create service prototypes to test and validate ideas.

- **Implementation**: Launch the service in the market and monitor its performance.

3.2.2 Personalization

Service personalization can significantly increase customer satisfaction. This includes the ability to tailor the service to individual customer preferences, offering customized options and recommendations based on past behavior.

3.3 Testing and Validation

3.3.1 Pilot Testing

Before launching a new service on a large scale, it is useful to conduct pilot tests to evaluate the service's effectiveness and identify any issues. This can include launching the service in a limited geographic area or with a selected group of customers.

3.3.2 Evaluation of Results

Analyze the results of pilot tests to identify areas for improvement and make necessary adjustments. This includes collecting customer feedback and analyzing performance metrics.

3.4 Implementation and Monitoring

3.4.1 Service Implementation

Service implementation requires detailed planning and effective resource management. This includes staff training, preparation of marketing materials, and setup of support systems.

3.4.2 Continuous Monitoring

Continuously monitor service performance and collect customer feedback to identify any issues and make ongoing improvements. This includes using key metrics such as customer satisfaction, retention, and adoption rates.

3.5 Innovation and Continuous Improvement

3.5.1 Service Innovation

Continuous innovation is essential to maintain competitiveness and meet evolving customer needs. This includes introducing new features, adopting emerging technologies, and exploring new business models.

3.5.2 Feedback Loop

Establish a continuous feedback loop between the company and customers to gather input and ideas for service improvement. This can include regular surveys, discussion groups, and customer data analysis.

3.6 Impact Evaluation

3.6.1 Measuring Success

Evaluate the impact of the new service or improvements through key performance indicators (KPIs). These metrics can include sales growth, market share, customer satisfaction, and return on investment (ROI).

3.6.2 Return on Investment Analysis

Calculate ROI to determine if the investment in the new service has generated positive value for the company. This includes analyzing the costs and benefits associated with the service.

4. Case Study: Example of Success in Creating an Effective Service

4.1 Case Study Context

Describe the business context and challenges faced by the company before market research. This includes an overview of the target market, competitors, and relevant trends.

4.2 Market Research Approach

Describe the approach used by the company to conduct market research. This includes the choice of methodology, data collection, and result analysis.

4.3 Interpretation of Results

Illustrate how the company interpreted market research results to identify customer needs and preferences. This includes data analysis and formulation of key insights.

4.4 Service Development and Implementation

Describe the process of developing and implementing the new service based on market research results. This includes service design, pilot tests, and large-scale implementation.

4.5 Results and Impact

Present the results obtained from implementing the new service, highlighting key performance metrics and ROI. This includes evaluating customer satisfaction, sales growth, and overall business impact.

Interpreting market research results and creating an effective service are interconnected processes fundamental to business success. Accurate and contextualized data analysis can provide valuable insights, while a strategic approach to service design and implementation ensures that customer needs are optimally met. Adopting continuous innovation practices and improvement based on customer feedback is essential to maintain competitiveness and respond to evolving market dynamics.

6. Implementation of Corrective Actions, Evaluation of Results, and Service Monitoring and Updating in Market Research

1. Introduction

Market research does not end with data analysis and result interpretation. The true value of research emerges when the results are translated into concrete actions that can improve products, services, and business strategies. This document provides a comprehensive guide on implementing corrective actions, evaluating results, and monitoring and updating the service, ensuring that decisions based on market research lead to real and sustainable improvements.

2. Implementation of Corrective Actions

2.1 Identifying Areas for Improvement

2.1.1 Gap Analysis

Gap analysis involves identifying discrepancies between customer expectations and current service performance. This process helps focus corrective actions on areas needing urgent improvement.

Steps in Gap Analysis:

- **Collect Feedback**: Use surveys, interviews, and reviews to gather feedback on service weaknesses.

- **Compare with Standards**: Compare current performance with industry standards and customer expectations.

- **Prioritize Gaps**: Rank gaps based on their importance and impact on the customer.

2.1.2 Root Cause Analysis

After identifying the gaps, it is essential to

analyze the underlying causes to develop effective corrective actions. This may include analyzing internal processes, resources, and staff competencies.

Tools for Root Cause Analysis:

- **Ishikawa Diagrams**: Used to identify the main causes of a problem.

- **Process Analysis**: Detailed review of processes to identify inefficiencies and friction points.

- **Discussion Groups**: Involving staff to gain insights into the operational causes of problems.

2.2 Developing Corrective Actions

2.2.1 Action Planning

Once the causes of the problems are identified, the next step is to plan specific corrective actions. These actions must be targeted, practical, and achievable.

Components of an Action Plan:

- **Specific Objectives**: Define clear and measurable objectives for each corrective action.

- **Required Resources**: Identify the resources (human, financial, technological) needed to implement the actions.

- **Responsibilities**: Assign specific responsibilities to team members.

- **Timelines**: Establish realistic deadlines for the implementation of actions.

2.2.2 Stakeholder Involvement

Involving stakeholders is crucial to ensure that corrective actions are supported and successfully implemented. This includes involving employees, managers, and, in some cases, customers.

Strategies for Engaging Stakeholders:

- **Transparent Communication**: Inform stakeholders about the action plans and expected benefits.

- **Collaboration**: Involve stakeholders in the process of developing corrective actions.

- **Continuous Feedback**: Collect and incorporate stakeholder feedback during implementation.

2.3 Implementing Actions

2.3.1 Execution of the Plan

The execution phase requires careful management to ensure that corrective actions are implemented as planned. This includes managing resources, overseeing progress, and resolving any problems that arise.

Key Activities in Plan Execution:

- **Resource Allocation**: Ensure that necessary resources are available and properly allocated.

- **Progress Monitoring**: Use project management tools to track progress against established timelines.

- **Problem Resolution**: Address any obstacles or deviations from the plan promptly.

2.3.2 Training and Support

Training and supporting staff are essential to ensure that corrective actions are effectively implemented. This can include training on new procedures, introducing new technologies, and providing ongoing support.

Elements of a Training Program:

- **Training Sessions**: Workshops and seminars to transfer the necessary skills.

- **Educational Materials**: Manuals, video tutorials, and other support materials.

- **Continuous Assistance**: Technical and operational support during and after implementation.

3. Evaluation of Results

3.1 Defining Evaluation Criteria

3.1.1 Performance Metrics

Evaluating the results of corrective actions requires defining key performance indicators (KPIs) that can measure the effectiveness of the actions taken.

Examples of KPIs:

- **Customer Satisfaction**: Measured through feedback surveys and Net Promoter Score (NPS).

- **Response Time**: Average time to resolve customer issues.

- **Customer Loyalty Rate**: Percentage of repeat customers.

- **Operational Efficiency**: Cost reduction and productivity increase.

3.1.2 Evaluation Objectives

Evaluation objectives must be clear and aligned with business goals. This includes identifying the specific aspects to improve and the expected outcomes.

Defining Objectives:

- **Specific**: Clear and detailed objectives.

- **Measurable**: Quantitative indicators to assess progress.

- **Achievable**: Realistic objectives based on available resources.

- **Relevant**: Aligned with business

strategy.

- **Time-bound**: Defined deadlines for achieving the objectives.

3.2 Data Collection

3.2.1 Collection Methods

Use appropriate data collection methods to monitor performance metrics and evaluate the effectiveness of corrective actions. This can include surveys, interviews, operational data analysis, and direct observations.

Data Collection Methods:

- **Surveys and Questionnaires**: Collect direct feedback from customers.

- **Interviews and Focus Groups**: Qualitative insights into customer experiences.

- **Operational Data Analysis**: Monitoring

operational and financial metrics.

- **Direct Observation**: Direct evaluation of customer interactions.

3.2.2 Data Management

Ensure that collected data is properly managed, securely stored, and accessible for analysis. This includes using data management systems and implementing data governance practices.

Data Management Practices:

- **Data Management Systems**: Use of databases and data analysis software.

- **Data Security**: Measures to protect sensitive data.

- **Accessibility**: Ensure that data is easily accessible for analysis and reporting.

3.3 Analyzing Results

3.3.1 Comparative Analysis

Compare the obtained results with the evaluation objectives and performance metrics to determine the effectiveness of corrective actions. This includes analyzing trends and variations over time.

Steps in Comparative Analysis:

- **Comparison with Objectives**: Check if evaluation objectives were achieved.

- **Trend Analysis**: Identify patterns and trends in collected data.

- **Variation Assessment**: Analyze variations in performance metrics.

3.4 Reporting and Communicating Results

Presenting the evaluation results in detailed

reports is essential for effectively communicating conclusions and recommendations. These reports should be clear, concise, and action-oriented.

Elements of Evaluation Reports:

- **Executive Summary**: Overview of main results and recommendations.

- **Detailed Analysis**: In-depth analysis of performance metrics, trends, and conclusions.

- **Charts and Graphs**: Use data visualizations to make results more understandable.

3.4.2 Executive Presentations

In addition to written reports, executive presentations are useful for communicating results to decision-makers and key stakeholders. These presentations should highlight key points in a visual and persuasive manner.

Characteristics of Executive Presentations:

- **Clarity and Conciseness**: Direct communication of main conclusions.

- **Visual Support**: Use slides with charts, diagrams, and tables to illustrate results.

- **Q&A Sessions**: Opportunities to clarify doubts and receive immediate feedback.

4. Service Monitoring and Updating

4.1 Implementing a Monitoring System

4.1.1 Defining Monitoring Metrics

After implementing corrective actions, it is essential to establish a continuous monitoring system to evaluate performance maintenance and detect new improvement opportunities.

Monitoring Metrics:

- **Continuation of Performance Metrics**: Maintain monitoring of the same metrics used in the initial evaluation.

- **Early Warning Indicators**: Identify early signs of emerging problems or negative trends.

- **Metric Updates**: Modify or add new metrics based on evolving market needs and operational conditions.

4.1.2 Monitoring Tools

Use technological tools and specialized software to automate the monitoring process and collect real-time data. These tools can include customer relationship management (CRM) software, reporting dashboards, and online feedback systems.

Advantages of Monitoring Tools:

- **Timeliness**: Receive updated data in real-time.

- **Automation**: Reduce manual work in data collection and analysis.

- **Predictive Analytics**: Ability to forecast future trends based on historical data.

4.2 Continuous Evaluation

4.2.1 Evaluation Cycle

Monitoring should be integrated into a continuous cycle of evaluation and improvement, allowing the company to quickly adapt to changing market conditions and customer needs.

Phases of the Continuous Evaluation Cycle:

- **Regular Monitoring**: Periodically update data and monitor performance.

- **Data Analysis**: Interpret new data to identify trends or anomalies.

- **Repeating Corrective Actions**: If necessary, implement new corrective actions based on new data.

4.2.2 Strategic Adaptation

Use monitoring results to adapt business strategies in response to market dynamics. This can include product updates, changes in marketing strategies, or process optimization.

4.3 Service Updating

4.3.1 Update Cycle

The service should undergo a continuous update cycle to maintain relevance and competitiveness in the market. This cycle can be driven by market research results and customer feedback.

Components of the Update Cycle:

- **Release of New Features**: Introduction of new features or improvements to the existing service.

- **Customer Feedback**: Evaluate customer feedback to identify areas needing improvement.

- **Technological Updates**: Adoption of new technologies or improvement of existing infrastructure.

4.3.2 Change Management

Managing change during service updates is essential to minimize negative impact on internal and external stakeholders. This can include staff training, transparent communication, and ongoing support.

Strategies for Change Management:

- **Training and Development**: Ensure staff are prepared for the implementation of changes.

- **Clear Communication**: Inform internal and external stakeholders about the reasons and benefits of updates.

- **Continuous Support**: Provide assistance during and after implementation to resolve issues and answer questions.

5. Conclusions

The implementation of corrective actions, evaluation of results, and monitoring and updating of services represent critical phases in the lifecycle of market research. These processes not only allow for addressing identified gaps and improving business performance but also for maintaining competitiveness in the market and continuously meeting customer needs. Adopting strategic approaches and effective methodologies for each of these phases is essential to ensure the long-term success of the company and maintain a competitive advantage in the increasingly dynamic and complex global market.

7. Glossary of Market Research Terms

1. **Market Research**: A systematic process of collecting, analyzing, and interpreting data relevant to understanding a market, including customers, competitors, and the environment.

2. **Market Analysis**: A detailed study of market dynamics to identify trends, opportunities, and threats.

3. **Market Segmentation**: Dividing the market into homogeneous groups of consumers with similar characteristics to facilitate targeted marketing strategies.

4. **Target Market**: Specific group of consumers to whom a product or service is aimed to maximize marketing effectiveness.

5. **SWOT Analysis**: Evaluation of a

company's Strengths, Weaknesses, Opportunities, and Threats to understand its competitive position.

Research Methods

1. **Research Methodology**: Approach and strategy adopted to collect and analyze research data.

2. **Quantitative**: Research methods based on numerical and measurable data, used to confirm market hypotheses and trends.

3. **Qualitative**: Research methods focused on deep understanding of consumer motivations, behaviors, and perceptions.

4. **Focus Group**: Guided group discussion to gather detailed opinions on a product or service.

5. **Interview**: Structured or semi-structured conversation to gather detailed information from key individuals.

Research Techniques

1. **Survey**: Data collection method based on standardized questions sent to a sample of individuals.

2. **Time Series Analysis**: Examination of data variations over time to identify patterns and trends.

3. **Cluster Analysis**: Statistical technique to identify groups of individuals with similar behaviors.

4. **Regression Analysis**: Assessment of causal relationships between variables to predict market behavior.

Tools and Technologies

1. **Data Analysis Software**: Platforms to manage, analyze, and visualize large volumes of research data.

2. **CRM (Customer Relationship Management)**: System to manage customer interactions, contact data, and behavior analysis.

3. **Dashboard**: Visual tool to monitor real-time key performance metrics.

4. **GIS (Geographic Information System)**: Software to analyze and visualize geographic data useful for market segmentation.

Metrics and Indicators

1. **Net Promoter Score (NPS)**: Metric to measure customer satisfaction and loyalty.

2. **Market Share**: Percentage of market held by a company or product compared to the total market.

3. **ROI (Return on Investment)**: Measures the return of an investment in a marketing campaign or business initiative.

4. **Conversion Rate**: Percentage of website visitors or contacts who complete a desired action.

Key Concepts

1. **Buyer Persona**: Semi-fictional representation of ideal customers based on demographic and behavioral data.

2. **Competitive Analysis**: Detailed study of competitors' strengths and weaknesses to identify competitive advantages.

3. **Brand Equity**: Commercial value derived from consumer perception, brand recognition, and trust.

4. **Customer Journey**: Path that a customer follows from awareness of the company to purchase and beyond.

Analysis and Interpretation

1. **Data Analysis**: Process of critically examining collected data to identify patterns and trends.

2. **Results Interpretation**: Research phase where data is analyzed to extract insights and recommendations.

3. **Benchmarking**: Comparing a company's or product's performance against industry standards or competitors.

4. **Customer Feedback**: Opinions, comments, and ratings provided by customers on their experience with a product or service.

Research Process

1. **Research Planning**: Defining objectives, methodologies, and resources needed to conduct effective market research.

2. **Research Execution**: Implementation of data collection methodologies, including sample management and information gathering.

3. **Results Analysis**: Processing and

interpreting collected data to formulate conclusions and recommendations.

4. **Final Report**: Detailed document summarizing research findings and recommended actions.

Communication Tools

1. **Executive Presentation**: Visual communication of research results for high-level decision-making.

2. **Research Report**: Written document including details on methodologies, collected data, analysis, and conclusions.

3. **Summary of Findings**: Concise overview of key points and research recommendations.

Index

1. Introduction pg.4

2. Defining Research Objectives pg.14

3. Identification of the Target Audience in Market Research pg.28

4. Choosing Research Methodology and Data Collection and Analysis pg.47

5. Interpretation of Results and Creation of an Effective Service pg.70

6. Implementation of Corrective Actions, Evaluation of Results, and Service Monitoring and Updating in Market Research pg.85

7. Glossary of Market Research Terms
pg.104

www.ingramcontent.com/pod-product-compliance
Lightning Source LLC
Chambersburg PA
CBHW071937210526
45479CB00002B/719